A Place to Stand

INDIANA UNIVERSITY POETRY SERIES

EDITOR: SAMUEL YELLEN

A Place to Stand

David Wagoner

INDIANA UNIVERSITY PRESS

BLOOMINGTON

1958

The poems "An Anthem for Man," "Credo Adoration" (1954); "Lines for a Dangerous Day," "The Crisis," "Epitaph," "The Coronation" (1956); "Murder Mystery," "Song at the End of Winter," "The Migration," "Elegy for a Distant Relative," "The Man from the Top of the Mind" (1957); "Words Above a Narrow Entrance," "To My Friend Whose Parachute Did Not Open," "A Warning to My Love," and "The Recognition" (1958), copyrighted in the respective years shown by *Poetry*. "Yesterday," "Admonition," "Memento Mori," and "Terminus" appeared in *Botteghe Oscure* XIII (1954); and "The Feast," "All Souls' Day," "The Hero with One Face," "Part Song," and "The Fallen" appeared in *Botteghe Oscure* XVIII (1956). "Lullaby through the Side of the Mouth" appeared in *The Yale Review* (1956), copyrighted by the Yale University Press. "Pause" (1953) and "Spring Song" (1956) appeared in *New World Writing* in the respective years shown, and copyrighted by the New American Library of World Literature, Inc. "Gift of a Mirror to a Lady," "Tan Ta Ra, cries Mars," and "News from the Court" appeared in *New Poems No. 2* (1957), copyrighted by Ballantine Books, Inc. "The Eye of the Storm," "The Balance," "Lament for the Very Few" appeared in *Prairie Schooner* (1958).

LIBRARY OF CONGRESS CATALOG CARD NUMBER: 58-8121

MANUFACTURED IN THE UNITED STATES OF AMERICA

For C. K. and S. K.

CONTENTS

A Place to Stand

A Place to Stand

On ancient maps, they stood,
Explorers, cartographers—
Between the dew-lapped god
Of the wind with an icy beard
And the arrow etched at north—
And panicked among the stars,
And tried the sun, and heard
The kraken plunging south.

They said, "Where are we now?"
But whirlpools turned the sea,
Swallowed and uttered land,
And flames cracked at the bow.
What solid geometry
Could guide their astrolabe?
Which latitude of the mind
Could cast them on the web?

They watched, on every shore,
Gargoyle and griffon rise,
Clawing the parchment air,
Scaling the dark for miles;
Saw the whole ocean poured
Like separate waterfalls
Down the corners of the world,
The corners of their eyes.

We ask, "Where are those ships?"
Keeled over on a chart.
"What lies around us, since
They foundered on old maps?"

The whirling continents,
The sky seen through a hole,
The stars flashing apart—
What master calls them real?

To My Friend Whose Parachute Did Not Open

Thrown backwards first, head over heels in the wind
Like solid streamers from the wing to tail,
You counted whatever pulses came to mind—
The black, the bright—and at the third, you pulled,
Pulled savagely at the ring clenched in your hand.

Down the smooth slope of your trajectory,
Obeying physics like a bauble of hail,
Thirty-two feet per second per second hurled
Toward treetops, cows, and crouching gravity
From the unreasonable center of the world,

You saw the cords trail out from behind your back,
Rise up and stand, tied to a piece of cloth
Whose edges wobbled, but would not spread wide
To borrow a cup of air and hold you both.
O that tall shimmer whispered you were dead.

You outraced thought. What good was thinking then?
Poor time—no time for plunging into luck
Which had, like your whirling, weightless flesh, grown thin.
I know angelic wisdom leaped from your mouth,
But not in words, for words can be afraid:

You sang a paean at the speed of sound,
Compressed miraculous air within your head
And made it fountain upward like a cowl.
And if you didn't, then you struck the ground.
And if you struck the ground, both of us died.

[13]

Song at the End of Winter

What are you wearing? "Snow."
Send two feet after two
On the glazed meadow
Past small fire and rue,
The turf and the bracken.

How are you feeling? "Frail."
As to a festival,
Bring kex and darnel
For turf and the fire's meal,
The rue and the bracken.

Where will you find them? "There."
Step softly where they are:
Ice is not stranger
Than bracken and small fire,
Than turf and rue.

Why are you waiting? "Love."
But is it warm enough
Below hawk and night-reeve
For bracken and the turf,
For small fire and rue?

And who will go with you? "One."
Yes, be white as the moon
Though the fields darken
With turf and bracken
Beyond rue and the small fire.

When shall I follow? "Now."
Like duck and drake we'll go
Round pond and silo,
Like bracken about rue,
Like turf in the small fire.

Murder Mystery

After the murder, like parades of Fools,
The bungling supernumeraries come,
Sniffing at footprints, looking under rugs,
Clasping the dead man with prehensile tools.
Lens against nose, false beard down to his knees,
The Hawkshaw enters, hoists his bag of tricks,
And passes out suspicion like lemonade:
"Where were you when the victim—" "In my room."
"Didn't you ask him whether—" "Double locks."
"Who switched the glasses on the—" "Crippled legs."
"Why were the ballroom curtains—" "Mad for years."
Then, tripping on clues, they wander through the house,
And search each other, frighten themselves with guns,
Ransack the kitchen and the sherry bins,
And dance in the bushes with the cats and dogs.

"Where is he?" says the Captain. "Nobody cares."
"We did it!" scream the butler and the maid.
"I did it too!" the jolly doctor cries.
And all join in—detective, counterfoil,
Ingénue, hero, and the family ghosts—
And, flapping like tongues, the trapdoors babble guilt,
The window-boxes, closets understairs,
Whatnots and chandeliers, grandfather clocks,
The sealed-up attic with its litter of bones—
All of them shake, and pour their secrets out.
And the happy party, bearing aloft the dead,
Handcuffed and drunk, go singing towards the jail;
Stage-hands roll up their sleeves, fold up the lawn,
Dismantle the hedges and the flowerbed,
Then follow, hauling the mansion, to confess.

Meanwhile, in another place—their figures cold,
Both turned to shadows by a single pain,
Bloodless together—the killer and the slain
Have kissed each other in the wilderness,
Touching soft hands and staring at the world.

Spring Song

O marvelous, our brave delight,
The sun stands in its hole,
And a warrior with a crocus wreath
Goes dancing for his soul,
Trailed closely by a harridan
Leading a milky cow.
Sigh, sigh for our lady,
The Mother of Fragments, now.

Delicate, on their hands and knees
Come Some from upper floors,
Leaping like hoppers, clocks, and toads
To celebrate all fours,
And twelve pocked maidens behind masks
Sing "Cuckolds All A-row."
Sigh, sigh for our lady,
The Mother of Fragments, now.

"I find no darkness in my head,
Alas," cries Bumbling Bill;
"O shake hands with the unenjoyed,"
Says lofty Mirabel.
"Simmer," sings the nightingale;
"Hokum," says the crow.
Sigh, sigh for our lady,
The Mother of Fragments, now.

"I dreamed that I was dead and gone,
Thank God," says Aunty Ann;
"Winter is over! Fold the beds,
And booze," cries Everyman.

"Bees," remarks the lily fly;
"Birdies," says the sow.
Sigh, sigh for our lady,
The Mother of Fragments, now.

O marvelous, O marvelous,
The widow of the weeds
Remembers feather, sun, and coast,
And plaits her bun with seeds,
And all the couriers of flesh
Snaffle themselves anew.
Sigh, sigh for our lady,
The Mother of Fragments, now.

The Eye of the Storm

After the battering night, rack and distress—
The waves like monuments above the mast,
Ruin in wind, the flocking of the stays,
And spray dark with the fallen dark—our ship
Careened from the haze, and came to calm at last.

In the storm's eye, all of us breathed again,
Felt the salt sunlight cleaving lip to lip,
Watched water shrink to a circle where the rain
Raised the horizon like a single shore.
We fished our luck out of the morning air.

What place was this? Whose garden in the sea?
What tiller of foam had plunged his rudder here?
We leaned against the taffrail, and we saw
Blossoms along the keel, an anchorage
For the sea-laid, star-crossed flowers of his rage.

The garland spread behind us and turned white,
And, like a wing, water to starboard rose
And hovered in long streamers, and its mate,
Grown huge to larboard, gathered for a stroke.
Slowly, the bowsprit lifted like a beak.

And while the mock suns wheeled from east to west,
Our lanyards tautened and gave way, and soared,
The skysail mounted to the gulls, the crest
Of the billowing deck came past us, and the strakes
Sprang from themselves like petals to the light,

And the deadlights skimmed astern, and the ripped shrouds
Fluttered beyond the yardarms toward the sun.
Here in the calm, here in our drying hoods,
Athwart the center and the furrow of noon,
We leaped above the water and cried, Love.

Elegy for a Distant Relative

This rubble of stained glass
Once glittered for a man
Who clapped at brightness
Till the dark ran
With inhuman noise, with inhuman noise.

This sand turning to sand
Was once a watercourse
Whereon the bucking stream
Pranced like a horse
To a light place, to a light place.

These knuckles underground
Were once a medlar tree
Whose branches and straight leaves
Wavered lightly
From a green haze, from a green haze.

And this eye turning to dust
Was once a man-at-tears
Whose pity was fastened
On the frozen stars
In a silent place, in a silent place.

Memento Mori

In my list of choices, death had not appeared.
The forest in my head, the scrambling words,
The stars and motes behind my eyes grew fierce
And fearsome before sleep. But none were black.
None loomed. In the woods were only birds to be feared;
In words, their loss; in stars, their merciless swords.
By the praise of my flesh, I could always pierce,
With clean ferocity, sleep's cul-de-sac.

I moved through the flaking air and had my say.
Time held its mirrors to my face: I looked,
And nose to nose, I stared my image down.
The rout of cretinous horrors in the night
Had left me cold but steady in my day.
What if the light was huge and steep? I knocked
Out of pride against the sun and dune
To make them speak. They did. I took no fright.

Angels and ashes seemed the freaks of age.
"Bring out your dead," I cried, and cocked my eye
To see the hillocks and the loam-beds stir.
Earth held. No bone broke out. No head of death
Sprang like a comet from the world at large,
Trailing its dark. "Poets refuse to die,"
I wrote on stone. Yet now, O God in Thy blur,
Who is it stuffs this murdering dust in my breath?

Words Above a Narrow Entrance

The land behind your back
Ends here: never forget
Signpost and weathercock
That turned always to point
Directly at your eyes;
Remember slackening air
At the top of the night,
Your feet treading on space.
The stream, like an embrace,
That swamped you to the throat
Has altered now; the briar
Rattling against your knees,
The warlock in disguise,
The giant at the root—
The country that seemed
Malevolence itself
Has gone back from the heart.

Beyond this gate, there lies
The land of the different mind,
Not honey in the brook,
None of the grass you dreamed.
Foresee water on fire,
And notches in a cloud;
Expect noise from a rock,
And faces falling apart.
The pathway underfoot,
Heaving its dust, will cross
A poisonous expanse
Where light knocks down the trees,
And whatever spells you took

Before, you will take anew
From the clack in the high wind.
Nothing will be at ease,
Nothing at peace, but you.

The Feast

Maimed and enormous in the air,
The bird fell down to us and died.
Its eyelids were like cleats of fire,
And fire was pouring from its side.

Beneath the forest and the ash
We stood and watched it. Beak to breast,
It floundered like a dying fish,
Beating its wings upon the dust.

What vague imbalance in our hearts
Leaned us together then? The frost
Came feathered from a sky of quartz;
Huge winter was our holy ghost.

O for light's sake, we turned to see
Waterglass forming on a stone;
A hag laughed under every tree;
The trees came slowly toppling down,

And all of the staring eyes were false.
Our jaws unhinged themselves, grew great,
And then we knelt like animals
To the body of this death, and ate.

Terminus

The taste of the day goes,
But we are left with tongues
In rooms nobody knows.

Shades draw the windows in;
The air waits in our lungs;
Around us, sounds begin

To quaver like our lives,
To dwindle like our songs.

Our hands, drawn up and down,
Shape nothing but ourselves:
We touch all that we own.

This was not so at noon
When nothing came by halves.
The bones forget soon.

A Warning to my Love

Born in my mouth, the naked beast leaned out
And bit the world at random for its meat.

Then, coveting all, it ate reflected light,
Drank shape and darkness from a richer throat,

And shuffled itself apart. O love, from Thing,
It turned into a man, lofted my tongue,

And cried blue language at the enemy:
All who were washed with sweeter milk than I.

Lusting, its flesh grew backward through my own,
Possessed it, leaped, and caught another skin,

Pierced it and crowed, strutted and beat my breast,
Then sprawled and tried the half-sleep of the lost,

And lies there yet, its seven sins at my lips,
Less dead than deadly. Waiting for you, perhaps.

Admonition

I'll have none of it, no, not even the wrath against enemies
That comes as easily as trick words or women to my hand;
Scratchback, spit in the soup, tits and tats: all of them lies
In the face of light whose look no hackwork can withstand.

I, with more cocks than hens, more seeds than holes,
Crawl through pastures where slate runs slantwise out of flaws,
Where the tough wind sticks its neck for nothing over the hills
To pierce me through the head. But no, no. I raise hooked
     claws.

It shall not be from rage nor from anger, this violence
Of eye and ear. Out of no known fakery it will cry:
What called me? Why? When will the flame and foam make
     sense?
How shall I quicken? Who are those animals? Where *am* I?

The Balance

Again, the marvels of the frost and field
Lie dumb: trees twice, the sky beside itself.
How shall I make one gesture serve for both?
To enter in, withdraw; be stark, or yield;
Run stricken into sanctity, or love.
Who takes my fashion, takes himself in half:
Rakehell and piddler in their common cloth
Come to a parting, and they cannot move.

Sweetness, that brutal enterprise, undoes
All coupling of the part and counterpart,
And what hangs bare, what slides out of my sight
Cannot be single. Flesh is what it was:
Merciful laggard to a touch; beneath,
The anarchy of choice that will not choose.
Going by darkness, coming false by light,
I sway at my center, balanced, drawing breath.

Credo Adoration

The Metaphor shall be god. The host
Of Sound beyond the hand and mind,
His son. And while light's fountains spume,
                    O grace of the blind,
Words shall triangulate the ghost,
Vision shall crucify the past.

Tree, grass, the bloom in dust,
Rise into flame, and the webs go
At once to the water's edge. All air
                    Falls into blue
Distance, lengthening as it must
Through caves where ax and bow were lost.

Crows in the branches call again;
The hornets mount; beneath the field,
Worms enter pebbles; and the hare,
                    Like wind, is filled
With barbs of sunlight; the brown crane
Stands among reeds, and takes the rain.

What was the truth that first appeared?
Sandstone, pounded, will make sand;
Stairs on the tower all drop off;
                    Elbow and hand
Are one in the dark; a milkweed sword
Will bleed, and seeds dry in the gourd;

Leaves vanish, and the slanting snow
Will stagger the lake; wind will burn;
Cocoons unravel like kite-string; love

In a curve lies born;
Snakes fly at a touch; out of the slow
Upheaval of clay-loam, the wands grow.

From *Spiritus Mundi* these descend:
Rock in the womb, Fire on the tongue,
Beast in the breast, Snake in the groin,
                    Rose in the dung,
And Bird in the tall clouds like the mind,
Sun at beginning, Sun at end,

The stretched man becoming Cross,
The Water quick, and Water dead,
Earth clutching Air like brick to quoin,
                    O Star in the head,
And Bone resurrected by clean moss,
The Tree of all, Sweetness in dross.

Creatures of light, give praise to blood;
Strike fields of aureoles in flesh
Where atoms spin themselves to doom,
                    Fountain and flash
In sight of ghost, loud son, and god,
Furthering flight as ashes should.

Call splendor from the wheel of days:
Desire's bright agony like gems
In the skull, whole brain gone numb
                    With harrowing dreams;
Accept, as Mother, soil and blaze,
Blaze, sea and wind; and give back praise.

All Souls' Day

An old, rich rain comes down
On the hummocks of the dead
And the side-slipped valley at dawn,

And all stones are one.
The rill-worn, pocked and angular
Moon-like rock on the wane

And the crushed shale
Are one in the rain that prays
Through land as a shell,

Through man (though dead
Or climbing through the whole light,
Or still-born and ended

In a moment's nautilus,
Or afraid, or limp in the skull
And taken, raptly, at a loss)

Or through the crossed grass like fire,
That other water, or the vine
Mounting the spread fir,

Or, Savior, the wilder flower,
Struck green beyond time and stamen:
Through flesh, through flare,

Or up the statued wind
Where the clouds stammer, naked,
Or flash to the light's wand

[33]

And sing; or through the curling,
Descending air come down to me,
Shut and starveling,

Here, through the stream of my lap,
Or the crescent glistening below my eyelid,
Or the cup at my lip,

Or through the loosening blood—
Rain, the rich, same rain for man,
For stone, for the grass blade,

And for the banked sky and valley now,
For me. Water is one water,
And birth its litany.

"*Tan Ta Ra, cries Mars . . .*"

—THOMAS WEELKES

"Clang!" goes the high-framed, feather-tufted gong. The mace
And halberd, jostled together, ring on the cobblestones,
While straight with the horde, blue flies and pieces of wings
Sail to the war. Owl's egg in mouth, the prophet sings
Glory from thumb-stirred entrails, glory from eagle-stains
And smoke, holding a cup of moly to his face.

"Blat!" go the thin-stemmed silver horns. High-tail and horse-
     behind,
Prouder than bustles, rise in the streets to prank
And fidget with the air. See, plumes at their ears,
The unicorns stumble—the ram-horned bugbears,
And the spears, all brassily crested, rank on jack-straw rank,
And the phalanx of bellies, and the rusty, bellying wind.

"Tan Ta Ra!" cries Mars, last in the callithumpian line
Where midgets, riding on dogs, squeak like his chariot wheels
And weep. Ta Ra to his majesty's knotted thighs and fists!
The knuckle-browed, crotch-guarded master of hosts,
The raggedy-hafted Mars goes forth, with stars on his heels,
To battle, twitching our dust behind him like a gown.

The Barrier

My body by itself at dawn
Rose like a groom
And walked into the field, and burned—
And, burning, staggered with its flame
Past blade and thicket, touching them,
Touching to splendor with its hand
The root, the spikelet, and the crown.

And turning with the wind, it made
Love to the land,
Scorched all that grew, all that had grown:
Leveled the carcanet of grain
And drove through leaf-mold, farther down,
Far as the blazing arm could reach,
And rose, and swept, and flared again.

Yet when my body with its fire
Fell against stone
Where time lay murdered by the shade—
(Why shall I curl? How may I touch?
Who echoes me to death?)—it turned
To strike that darkness like a dream,
And sang, and burned again, and burned.

Epitaph

I sing one for the Giantess:
Her ladyship is dead.
May God confound her till she humps
And hangs her cloudy head
(Though what man said that to her face,
He were a man indeed).

Old age, like hooks beneath the skin,
Has pulled her sinews off;
And while my bellybone can hold,
I shall take drink enough
To flood the memory of that bitch
Who called her hunger love.

She made me child and father, beast,
Mother, and Holy God,
All but a shape of love. I kept
Great bitterness in my head
While she grew up, grew down, grew fur,
Or froze upon a bed.

The slattern of the innocents
Has dropped to her reward.
May it be dampness, darkness, dirt,
Silence—all she abhorred,
All the retreats poor wretches sought
When skies fell at her word.

Today, my studs, there is no more
Lady and breast-fired kin.

The smear of birth has dried away
From netherlip and chin.
We owned each other's worst. Praise be,
Mine is no longer mine.

Lullaby through the Side of the Mouth

Goodnight, unlucky three. Mice at a feast
Go nibbling the grain away; the wrens
Fluff one another in the hollow post;
And moths are knuckling at the windowpanes.

O pray to the wall, pray to the billypan,
Render all praise to footboards and the sheets,
Call up the spiral mattress if you can:
But see, at your eyes, the counterclockwise lights.

Now you must sacrifice—first, to the dark,
Next, to the crippled underhalf of the mind—
Your faces, hearts, whatever does good work,
Before you come to the burrows at wit's end.

Once more, the holes lie open into dreams:
In one, a hairless tail; in one, a quill;
And, in a third, antennae with soft plumes.
Now put them on, dear Lust, my Love, poor Will.

May forefeet lift each kernel like a cup;
May beak and claw touch heaven under wings;
May the dust-flecked moth find every window up.
But those are joys. You will not dream such things.

The Hero with One Face

They chose me, not that I might learn,
But only because I was born,
And gave me amulets of clay,
Some armor, and a brief goodbye.

And at the threshold of the pool,
The looking-glass, the spoiled well,
The hole beneath the whirling tree,
I waited meekly. They called me.

I turned a corner, and was there,
Where all the other places are:
The other side of the cupped moon,
Oz, Heaven-Hell, and the Unknown.

I had too many purposes:
Although they hadn't said, "Find keys,
Find maidens, answers, and lost loves,"
I knew they wanted these themselves,

And I was bound to seek them all
Or be transformed, or die, or fall.
All the horned gods soared by and looked,
Hoping to stain my smallest act.

And there were beasts: three-headed dogs,
Gorgons, ghouls with whirligigs,
And dragons both alive and dead
For me to master, and I did.

[40]

I did, and O they brought Her in:
My Mother, the Queen upon a throne,
The Circe with a mouth to fill,
The witch already beautiful.

How could I know Her without pain?
I turned: there sat the evil King,
Betrayer, jealous brother, God.
I loved him much more than I should.

Then Glory rattled from a cloud,
The deaf-and-dumb rose up and cried,
Cripples came striding, golden fleece
Fell from the holy air like lace,

And broken curses rained, and time
Gave birth, gave birth, and returned home
Where all of the unmade desires
Are made at last. And I felt worse,

And I was elected to a boon,
A final wish for every man.
I chose what I was told to choose:
They told me gently who I was.

It scarcely mattered. I lay down
And ate the lotos, kissed my crown,
And gazed at Ozma, Beatrice,
And sighed, and was content with this.

But no—two-legged horses came,
Ogres, winds, and mothers-in-loam,
Provoked husbands with their wives,
Little people with long knives,

The shadows of the underworld;
And all my journey was recoiled,
Drawn back to the uneasy place
Where each benign beginning is.

Now, like Ulysses, master of
The world under, world above,
The world between—and one beyond
Which was not near enough to find—
I wait, and wonder what to learn:
O here, twice blind at being born.

The Migration

This is the trail. Or this.
Who made it? Animals.
Won't someone go to sleep?
Or must I be the first,
I who have eaten stones
Yet sung through the aimless miles?
Though children in the trees
Once glistened like ripe fruit,
Now each one climbs to hang.
Look, not even the mist
Around us will lie down.

Before he vanished again
My brother lost his foot;
My father staggered away
To die. What did they say?
Did no one else complain?
Those rags wearing the men,
All standing nose to nose
In the whitening air like sheep,
Have they decided? No.
Then I say somebody must:
Do we sleep, rot, or go?
I ask, but I'll decide.
Remember when we said
Let's put a freak in charge?
We didn't. But we shall.

I am that madman now,
Streaked in the face, one lip
Ruling the other lip,

And the left eye grown huge,
The forelock raised with fire,
Legs spinning into one,
My hands through the sky. I know
The way to the tumbling ditch,
The fork and the underfork—
We'll follow water down,
Drink it and be it, grow
Lengthy, till we reach
Exhaustion in the dark
Where the dismembered beasts
Before us melted and fell.
This, this is the trail.

Pause

Nearer than ever, night will come,
And shapes stand nearer in the sky,
And earth melt upward through the trees
Like air in shadow, air gone numb,

Like air turned over with a sigh,
Nearer than ever, all of these,
With star-dark, moon-dark in the mind,
And several silences nearby,

And ground-mist, aimless in the wake,
Turned over and over by the wind,
Farther than ever from the light,
And forms revolving till daybreak,

And mercy standing out of sight,
Still with itself and ill at ease,
And alcove in me for no sound,
And, nearer than ever, room for night.

The Fallen

In the slight dark, we stood
Slyly upon our bones;
Comfort came, and stayed.
The hands beside our hands
Shifted, took their ease
So lightly, we could smile
To touch them and to kiss.
The pond of flesh lay still.

But at near-dark, what rang
Around us like a choir
Grown violent with its song?
The people on the stair,
The rooms beneath the floor
Cried cadence, and we wept.
Our shadows took the air;
The face in the mirror gaped.

And then, at entire dark,
Everything ceased. Each hid
His nothing behind his back.
The impenetrable eyelid
Wavered and came down,
And dangling from mouth to mouth,
The ancient ghosts streamed in
To ravel strife and breath.

Our double chaos now
Turns upon silences,
Is swirled about a slow
Center, and ruined thus.

O daylight was our own,
But these are the states of night:
From ease, to the crying down,
Then vacancy outright.

Gift of a Mirror to a Lady

Take it, my dear. Keep it beneath your pillow,
Beneath the flax and feathers—all the uprooted—
Beneath the hair, the bone, the dream gone yellow.
But use it someday. See what you have hated.

Lift it. You will remember by this token
The landscape where our summer turned to fable:
There lies the larchtree with its crested lichen,
And past the gate, the wet scythe and the stubble.

Close to your eyelid, see the grapevine slacken
And die, the trellis alter; there in the silvered
Flatness of your mind, the earth will sicken,
Water be silent in the moss-filled culvert.

And birds you have never seen, gold-clawed and burning,
Will splash from the fallen branches, rise to flutter
The glass beside you, striking the air and staring.

Then shatter the mirror. It was made to shatter.

News from the Court

Summoned by love and heat and God knows what,
On the plush-filled stairway, raising his plushy feet,
(Silent, his lips as purple as his robes),
The King climbs to the Queen by candlelight.

Before his knees have knocked at the outer door,
Before his voice has lifted like a latch,
Before the ring-led fingers of the King
Have found bed-curtains flapping at a touch,

The news is trumped abroad through corridors
To the streets and sticks, earholes and buttresses,
From cup to spigot, rake to gutterstone,
And along the chancel through the bishop's nose:

Will it be prince, or princess, or still-birth?
What's the most regal answer to a bite?
How many fathoms deep is mother of pearl?
If the watchman says, "Ahem," how goes the night?

But secret in state, themselves conspirators,
Ageless Regina and the First of Shades
(The King, without the knavery of his lords,
The Queen, without lip-service from her maids)

Perform once more their ceremonious love
For love, for time, for rage they have never lost:
He riding on her field of the cloth of gold,
She striking again the history of his breast,

And the royal couple lie in a chronicle—
Despite the clucks and pennysheets in the town—
Strewn through each other like their images:
The orb, the scepter, and the whirling crown.

Part Song

So cool, so clear at noon,
The water moves along,
Loitering in its pools
Like the bequeathed air
In rooms where wind has gone.

The curved grass leans down
And wavers at the verge
As lithe as blown tendrils,
And, uncertain, water spills
Over the turned stone.

What am I now? Between
My hands the light lies bare
Or goes as the wind goes,
Into pools—or bending, trails
In water like a fin

Or, vanishing, moves on
To gather grass, to pose,
There, where the streams soon merge.
What was I once? Among
The eddies stones lie clean.

The spray sails like a rain
And vanishes; the moss
Grows darker than my eyes.
O what will I be? The pools
Lie still in the still noon.

The Man from the Top of the Mind

From immaculate construction to half death,
See him: the light bulb screwed into his head,
The vacuum tube of his sex, the electric eye.
What lifts his foot? What does he do for breath?

His nickel steel, oily from neck to wrist,
Glistens as though by sunlight where he stands.
Nerves bought by the inch and muscles on a wheel
Spring in the triple-jointed hooks of his hands.

As plug to socket, or flange upon a beam,
Two become one; yet what is he to us?
We cry, "Come, marry the bottom of our minds.
Grant us the strength of your impervium."

But clad in a seamless skin, he turns aside
To do the tricks ordained by his transistors—
His face impassive, his arms raised from the dead,
His switch thrown one way into animus.

Reach for him now, and he will flicker with light,
Divide preposterous numbers by unknowns,
Bump through our mazes like a genius rat,
Or trace his concentric echoes to the moon.

Then, though we beg him, "Love us, hold us fast,"
He will stalk out of focus in the air,
Make gestures in an elemental mist,
And falter there—as we will falter here

And turns in rage upon our horrible shapes—
When the automaton pretends to dream
Those nightmares, trailing shreds of his netherworld,
Who must be slaughtered backward into time.

Lines for a Dangerous Day

Piecemeal, the ruck of fall
Went by us—halves of trees,
The bodies of the birds—
And less of the field stood still
Than passed us in the air,
And all that passed made All
An Armageddon of light.
O straight from the grass he came
To marvel at his loss:
The tall, the standing King.

He came, and came to kill.
Hawthorn, shag, and thing,
Caught in the midst of flight,
Gave over, and our eyes
Became what they were not,
And nothing was the same.
Up from his crest of hooks
A daybreak rose and stayed,
A miracle of ire,
A sacrament of wrath—
O all those innocents
Withered and died the death.

He was there, and was thrice there,
And for our piteous sakes
We turned from reed to rod,
Daring this man's despair—
The ungovernable day of acts—
To have the Fall be done.

Then, with petal and stone
Around him like a pyre
He strode upon his shards.
We faced him, and we fell.

The Crisis

Daring annihilation at the heart,
I come to brightness, to the staves of fire,
Cast where the known world rises like a shore.
O father, here at the burning of my name,
I pray you: suffer the towering light,
Stay motionless, and do not cross my flame.

Between calamities on sea and earth
I cry my answer to your cloud of ice:
I have a face upon my chest; it sleeps,
Then wakes to fall through fathoms of my ghost;
I have a shade within my brow that leaps
From time past time, beyond your frozen coast.

O the forked oaktree planted at my birth
Is split upon the turning point of love.
I wait to be consumed where my life began,
My hands behind me, eyes on either blaze:
The heart's immediate fire against the bone,
The mind's impossible flare through paradise.

Lament for the Very Few

(for Jack, Herb, and John)

The yard was lovely rubble then,
All sticks and tassels, the wet leaves,
And grass gone haywire through the stones.
Sprawling among them with our lives,
We saw, like star-marks overhead,
The meeting of the flower and air,
The severance of the quick and dead:
Like rain, our eyes fell everywhere.

Thornledge and thicket made us friends
Because their lavishness became
The image of our straggling minds:
Beyond the spectrum—O the limb,
Pod, loosening arch, and wing,
Beetle-made-rainbow, the strewn sheaves,
The ravelled edge of everything—
Over the briar we tossed ourselves.

First came the sun and the parching wind,
And then the match, and now the smoke;
And order stamps upon the ground
Where the stiff rake has been at work.
And the sharp scythe, the hook and plough,
The hatchet and the pruning shears
Have thinned and heaped us separately
In the single-colored smoke of years.

Yesterday

Mistaken at dawn, I rose and took the sun.
My eyes looked out
On death in the weeds, and anger in the stone,
Remorse in the enormous oak, and doubt
In the shape of animals. I named them One.

Misled at noon, I walked unlike the rest.
My eyes looked past
The floodlit arenas of the groin and breast
Where strangers touched each other, at the vast
Assassinated throngs. I called them blest.

Misinformed at dusk, I chanced upon a love.
My eyes looked through
The hazy flesh at the heart's root, saw the rough
Fibre, my enemy, rise and rise anew,
And fall, and brim with blood. I thought it enough.

Mislaid at night, I turned on a hard bed.
O my eyes looked back
To the day and forth to the easy daylight fled
From my sight forever, to the clamped and flaunted black
Of thing, and man, and love. I called them dead.

Misnaming them dead, I slept. But woke in pain
And found my eyelids streamed with light again.

An Anthem for Man

I sing the stone that is not stone: the unlocked,
Disunioned crag of flesh, perdurable
As the sun's fist; whose elements are rocked
And slammed to sleep and shattered, and made whole.

I sing the weed that is not weed: the uprooted,
Thornless shape with a scattering of seed
To the cast wind; whose green and gold are mated
In one bloom, healed to one stricken blood.

I sing the beast that is not beast: the unhorned,
Hoofless bullock with a flaming eye
And raging mind; whose animus is turned
Against pain and its intolerable outcry.

I sing the god that is not God: the unblessed,
Tangible image with a world to fathom
Or damn; whose tears, like light, have washed
The broad face of the darkness and been nothing.

I sing the man that is all man: all these,
The stone, marred weed, the beast and god, yet none
While his muck sings, and time streams from his thighs,
And he, almighty, makes worlds with his tongue.

The Coronation

From the principality of loss,
O light and air,
See, the sweet body has returned—
King of the worlds—
To plant, and plume, and spire,
And the flourish of darkness,
And the flood, and the clamoring mind:
O see, from core to fire,
The dense glory, and the quick-lime of the bone,
The luminous skeleton
Draws breath,
Draws daylight, the mark of kind,
Inner and outer meeting in its mouth,
By day, with day in its hands,
The fingers rising across the brow,
The brow gathering to its headlands,
Chaos enclosed again,
And the storm gone:
O beautiful king of flaws,
O shape and stream,
Welcome, welcome to the throne.

The Recognition

I recognize myself, but not by sight,
Night-mark, or hand:
By sense, I am no more—neither the sun,
Nor the ravening, bone-struck mass in archaic space,
Goat-man or hound,
Nor the scrag-at-worship, stone-is-my-kin
Redeemer, scoring the tatters of his face.
I am no longer skin:
It knows far better what it was, than is,
Saying, "Whose taste? Whose tracery is this?"

Even my mind, that widower of light,
The past-and-never-the-present singleness,
Old knockabout,
Has sprung from its matter, flaming from dark to clout.
I am no longer vision. Though I see,
The worlds are doubling in my eyes:
The two-in-one, the twice, the in-and-out,
Spinning impossibly
Across the mottled straits of the unknown
To say, "Whose thought is this? Which is my own?"

I had a name; and now I have a name:
I arch between them, neither lost nor found.
Out of the kneeling ground,
Down from the beating sky the two words came;
But turned at the wrist and turned in the skull's night,
My sensual abstract, my rib at reason,
I am no more.
This body and this thought
Are strangers saying, "What has filled us now?"
O love, I recognize myself by you.

[61]

The First Word

There had been sounds before: the trumpeting snout,
The crackling of the earth.
The trees had spoken for a million years;
Water had fallen; the great bees, gesturing,
Droned in their hollows, crying what was sweet.
Deep in his cave, he heard them; and his throat
Clouded with shapes and storms.
What could he do, whose tongue was but a thing?

Was it death-noise first? Or the would-be thunderer,
Man-become-weather, shouting at the sky?
Or naked and hungry, mad, nibbling at fur,
The one who heard the Others growl as they bled,
And dreamed his terrible name?
Or did his fingers bring such bitterness
From world to lip
He cried aloud to see them come again?

The sunlight blazed outside, purple and green
On the stones and fern-leaves. Did he call it *day*?
No, but he raised his eyes.
The roof of his mouth was burning like the sun;
The water beneath his tongue had run away,
And Another stood at the entrance like a god.
A voice stirred in the wilderness of his head.
Was it *yes* or *no*? Was it *you* or *me* he said?

ERRATUM

The stanza on page 53 should read:

When the automaton pretends to dream

And turns in rage upon our horrible shapes--

Those nightmares, trailing shreds of his netherworld,

Who must be slaughtered backward into time.

DATE DUE